Unfold Your Golden Wings

Using Past Lives, Dreams, and Soul Travel
to Unravel the Mysteries of God

Unfold Your Golden Wings

Using Past Lives, Dreams, and Soul Travel
to Unravel the Mysteries of God

Robert Marsh

ECKANKAR
Minneapolis

Unfold Your Golden Wings: Using Past Lives, Dreams, and Soul Travel to Unravel the Mysteries of God

Copyright © 2003 ECKANKAR

All rights reserved. No part of this book may be reproduced, stored in a retrieval system, or transmitted in any form by any means, whether electronic, mechanical, photocopying, recording, or otherwise, without prior written permission of Eckankar.

The terms ECKANKAR, ECK, EK, MAHANTA, SOUL TRAVEL, and VAIRAGI, among others, are trademarks of ECKANKAR, P.O. Box 27300, Minneapolis, MN 55427 U.S.A.

Printed in U.S.A.

Edited by Joan Klemp, Anthony Moore, and
Mary Carroll Moore

Illustrations by
Rose Wise
Ed Parkinson
(layout, design, and illustration by Ed Parkinson,
copyright © Ed Parkinson/Design Desk and their licensors)

Publisher's Cataloging-in-Publication
(Provided by Quality Books, Inc.)

Marsh, Robert, 1955–
   Unfold your golden wings : using past lives, dreams, and soul travel to unravel the mysteries of God / Robert Marsh.
   p. cm.
   LCCN 2003102522
   ISBN 1-57043-196-5

   1. Eckankar (Organization) 2. Spiritual life—Eckankar (Organization) I. Title.

BP605.E3M365 2003   299'.93
                                QBI03-200201

The opinions expressed in this publication are those of the writer and not necessarily those of Eckankar or the Living ECK Master, Sri Harold Klemp.

∞ The paper used in this publication meets the minimum requirements of the American National Standard for Information Sciences—Permanence of Paper for Printed Library Materials, ANSI Z39.48-1984.

"Open your wings, and you will know who you are." This is the whole point of the path of ECK and these teachings. Open your wings means simply to open your state of consciousness, and then you will know who and what you are.

> —Harold Klemp,
> *The Secret of Love,*
> Mahanta Transcripts, Book 14

Contents

1. Soul Exists Because God Loves It 1
2. Soul Is Going Home to God 5
3. Soul Must Exercise Its Own Creativity to Find God 11
4. Using the Spiritual Exercises of ECK to Connect with the Holy Spirit 15
5. Accepting the Assistance of the Living ECK Master 21
6. Uncovering the Totality through Eckankar 27
7. Finding Divine Guidance in Everyday Life 33
8. The History and Purpose of Eckankar 39
9. Some Frequently Asked Questions 47
10. A Spiritual Exercise to Try at Home 53
11. Next Steps 55
12. The Age-old Quest for Divine Love and Spiritual Freedom 57

1
Soul Exists Because God Loves It

Ancient Spiritual Laws

Abraham Lincoln once said, "Every man over forty is responsible for his face."

In a humorous way he was saying that what appears on the surface is an accurate reflection of what lies underneath. If we want to change our outer circumstances, we must first make the necessary changes within.

That wise American president understood an ancient law.

There are many ancient laws just like this one which, if properly understood, can bring deep satisfaction to our life here on earth. For example, Lincoln also noted that, "Most folks are about as happy as they make up their minds to be." In other words, we are each the captain of our own ship. From a spiritual standpoint, all we need is the right kind of training to sail safely through uncharted waters, to discover new horizons and to have many new and fulfilling experiences.

Eckankar is a study of the ancient spiritual laws and the way they affect our lives.

Your Reality as Soul

When Alexander the Great was engaged in his remarkable campaign of conquest in foreign lands, he often sought advice from mystics, seers, and wise men. He wanted to know why his many victories in battle did not bring him the satisfaction he craved. When word came to him that the famous philosopher Diogenes was living some miles from his camp, he set off to visit the old man. As he rode up he saw Diogenes down on his knees, sorting through a pile of human bones. Alexander sat on his horse for some time, trying to figure out what the old guy was up to. At last, overcome by curiosity, he got down from his horse and came over. Diogenes continued with his task, saying, "I am looking for the bones of your father, but I am unable to distinguish them from those of his slaves."

Stripped of our outer covering, we are all equal as Soul. Diogenes knew this. He also knew that, without a proper understanding of this principle, Alexander would steer ambitiously from one conquest to another but achieve nothing of substance.

This is a central tenet of Eckankar—a basic spiritual law, if you like. True fulfillment can come only when we realize our nature as Soul. Not the body, not the mind, not the subconscious, but Soul. There are a thousand teachings on earth today but few have retained a clear focus on this simple principle.

Soul is a spark of God, an atom of the Absolute, and as such is imperishable and eternal. What is more, It exists only because of God's love. Without that love, we would cease to be.

Finding the True Teacher

The ancient laws are easy to understand, but the real skill lies in seeing them at work in our daily life. This often means finding a teacher with a proven track record, heeding his words, and putting the knowledge we have learned into practice.

When the well-known Italian composer Pietro Mascagni was working in his studio one afternoon, an organ-grinder began to ply his trade in the street below. The noise was disturbing the composer—since the tune was being played at half the correct speed. So he went down to the organ-grinder and said, "I am Mascagni. Let me show you how to play this music correctly." The following day Mascagni saw the same organ-grinder at work, but this time he had a sign hanging from his organ. It read, "Pupil of Mascagni."

Everybody wants to associate with a great teacher, but few are willing to undertake the disciplines involved. They put up a sign to show their allegiance but, other than that, nothing has changed. So their lives grind on as they did before.

There are many strengths to Eckankar. One of the most important is that its spiritual leader—known as the Mahanta, the Living ECK Master—is able to guide and protect each of his students at any time, no matter where they happen to be.

Your Purpose in Life

If Soul exists because God loves It, then why are we here on earth? The answer: purification. It is only through our experiences here in these material worlds—over many, many lifetimes—that we gain the maturity and awareness needed to return to our true home in the high worlds of God, the worlds of Light and Sound. How quickly or how slowly you go is entirely up to you. Each religion on earth today is designed to provide Soul in the human form with an understanding of one or more facets in the awesome spectrum of truth.

No matter what religion you follow, or even if you follow none in particular, you are on your way back home to God. Eckankar provides a way to accelerate this process.

When the explorers Lewis and Clark were making their way across North America in the early nineteenth century, charting unknown territory as they went, they had many adventures together. On one occasion Clark went on ahead and left a note in a prominent tree for Lewis to collect. However, when they finally met up, Clark was mystified to learn that Lewis had failed to find the tree. It was nowhere to be seen. After puzzling over this conundrum for some time they realized what had happened: a beaver had eaten through the tree and dragged it into a river.

The world keeps changing around us. We can follow the instructions left by those who have gone before us, but they often prove useless. Most Souls will only succeed in their quest by finding a living spiritual guide, someone who knows who you are, where you are going, and the route you must take to get there. This route is unique to each individual.

2
Soul Is Going Home to God

Soul Travel

When Paul Twitchell first wrote about Eckankar in the mid–twentieth century, very few knew about out-of-body travel. Today most people are familiar with the concept. As the Living ECK Master of the time, Paul Twitchell taught a special kind of out-of-body movement known as Soul Travel. He defined it as "movement from one state of consciousness to another." By teaching the dynamics of Soul Travel, some basic spiritual laws, and a set of proven techniques for achieving a deep state of contemplation, he enabled many of

his students to advance into a much higher level of spiritual awareness.

Today many children in Western society are exposed to out-of-body concepts. For example, in one episode of *The Simpsons* (a family cartoon series), the little eight-year-old Lisa brought her father, Homer, to a New Age emporium to try out the sensory-deprivation tanks. This involved floating in warm water in a dark and silent container. After a while each of them had an out-of-body experience. Lisa learned what it was like to see life through the eyes of their family cat, while her dad—whose outlook on life was less adventurous—spent most of his time wondering when he was going to get back into his physical body.

Contemporary TV aside, actual Soul Travel helps both to purify one's consciousness and to reveal the reality of the worlds beyond.

The Journey of Soul

We each came from God, and we are making our way back home again. This vast educational journey takes many, many lifetimes in these lower worlds of time and space. Along the way, we incarnate into many different races, religions, and countries, learning more about the depth and wonder of creation. We are also learning to accept more of God's love.

This remarkable journey is fueled by the Law of Cause and Effect, also known as the Law of Karma. Our actions in each lifetime determine the kinds of experience we will undergo in later lives. By working through the consequences of our previous actions, we slowly mature as spiritual beings. Eventually we reach a point—a milestone in our unfoldment—where we recognize our exile from God and yearn to return to our true home. When we reach this crucial lifetime, we may change religion many times, try all kinds of esoteric paths and techniques, and even drive ourselves to distraction in an attempt to resolve the enigma of our own existence.

Many people in Eckankar today went through this kind of experience. They kept looking until they found the Living ECK Master.

In his book *The Hero with a Thousand Faces*, Joseph Campbell examines the features common to all great stories and legends. A hero sets off to find something of unique importance, faces a great many trials and perils, loses everything he possesses, lapses into despair, finds solace and renewal through selfless love, rekindles his initial vision, and then bounds forth in a courageous burst of energy to achieve his goal. These stories, which are found in every culture and civilization since the dawn of time, reflect the journey of Soul in the lower worlds.

You are the hero. You too are on a great journey. And you too must find the love, vision, and energy to achieve your spiritual goal.

The Sound Current

The Living ECK Master is sent by God to assist seekers on their journey home. He is the one who brings the selfless love which enables the hero to rekindle his inner vision. As the inner and outer teacher, he provides the guidance needed by the seeker to negotiate the difficulties and challenges in his sojourn here on earth. To detect and appreciate this subtle inner direction, we need only practice the Spiritual Exercises of ECK for about twenty minutes or so every day.

These exercises are based on the Light and Sound, the twin aspects of the Holy Spirit. The Light is familiar to most students of religion, but few are aware of the Sound and Its central importance for all who wish to move beyond their existing state of consciousness. If you have been blessed with an experience in the Light, then you know It is more than just a figure of speech. It is a living reality. The Sound, too, is an actual sound, heard through one's inner ears. When they first hear the Sound, many seekers think It must be an outer sound emanating from an unknown source, but when they go to investigate Its origin, it can't be found. Why? Because the Sound comes from within.

The Sound is the Music of God, the voice of the Absolute resonating through the worlds of creation. As the Mahanta, the Living ECK Master of today, Sri Harold Klemp has said:

> The Sound does not come as the voice of an awesome deity speaking to you. Instead, depend-

ing upon your level of consciousness during contemplation or in the dream state, It can come in the form of music, the different sounds of nature, or any number of ways.

For instance, you might hear It as the buzzing of insects, the twittering of birds, the tinkling of bells, or musical instruments. What it means is that, at this particular time, the Sound of God is entering into you to bring about the purification of Soul.

—The Art of Spiritual Dreaming

3
Soul Must Exercise Its Own Creativity to Find God

Why Truth Seems Difficult to Find

Surely this is too simple, you say? Well, yes and no. Truth *is* simple, but our minds generate complexity. We look too much to religious laws and rules and neglect the daily practice of simply *listening* to God. That is where truth lies.

God created Satan for a purpose. Known as the Kal by students of Eckankar, Satan has the task of misdirecting Soul. Satan cannot destroy or even modify truth, but he can disguise it in cunning and misleading ways.

A lovely Irish folktale illustrates the way this works. An old lady was wandering through the fields one afternoon when she heard a leprechaun tapping away behind a tree, making shoes. The leprechaun was so absorbed in his task that he didn't notice the woman creeping up on him. So the woman grabbed hold of his coat and said, "I've got you now!" The leprechaun agreed to pay the price of freedom, the location of his gold. The leprechaun led the old lady to where the pot of gold was buried in a field overgrown with bushes. But the woman needed to get a spade from home to retrieve the gold. So, before releasing the leprechaun, the old lady tied her red scarf on the bush where the gold was buried. When the woman came back to the field an hour later, breathless with excitement, her heart sank. Every bush had a red scarf tied to it.

This is why truth is often difficult to find.

Why Eckankar Is Special

As mentioned earlier, all religious teachings lead seekers to some understanding of truth. However, Eckankar differs from them in at least three important respects: First, it is always led by a living prophet, not just a scriptural text or an appointed leader. Second, it emphasizes the crucial importance of the Sound Current and Soul Travel in the conscious unfoldment of Soul. And third, it provides the ECK initiations to those who have earned them. These alone lead to the complete liberation of Soul.

Groucho Marx once joked that he would never join a club that would have him as a member. Many seekers are like this. Their painful experiences with groups which abused their trust, whether in this lifetime or in previous lives, have left many wary of religious organizations. They expect truth to come solely from within. Alas, life is not like this. Even a living spiritual prophet or Master needs an outer organization to disseminate his teachings. If he worked only from the inner planes, very few seekers would find him, and those who did would assimilate only a small part of his teaching. What is more, none would receive the outer initiation.

When he works from the inner planes, notably through the dream state, the Living ECK Master is known as the Mahanta. Just as Jesus had the Christ Consciousness and Gautama had the Buddha Consciousness, so the Living ECK Master has the Mahanta Consciousness. This high state of God Awareness enables him to move freely through the lower worlds and to guide sincere and dedicated seekers to the Soul Plane and beyond. It also enables him to be present spiritually at all times with each of his students and to assist them in their unfoldment.

The Creativity of Soul

Eckankar emphasizes an active life—not withdrawing from the world or retreating to a monastery or ashram. It is only by living fully that we harvest the experiences needed to promote our unfoldment. The ups and downs of daily life provide a rich and challenging environment in which to develop our spiritual creativity. This in turn expands our awareness and prepares us for entry into higher levels of consciousness.

Once we become aware of Divine Spirit—the ECK—in our lives, we begin to appreciate our own extraordinary potential and the vital role we can play as distributors or channels for this divine substance.

The creativity of Soul can lead to a happier family life, better and more fulfilling relationships, success in the workplace, the development of new skills, and many new avenues of spiritual expression.

Through his exceptional talents, the physicist Richard Feynman made many valuable contributions to the science of quantum mechanics. A warm and witty individual, he often spent time chatting with his students and toying with new ideas. One day, while sitting in the college cafeteria, he observed a student tossing a dinner plate into the air. As the plate went up in the air, he noticed how it wobbled. He had just been thinking about a longstanding problem in physics, the spinning of electrons, trying to figure out why they seemed to possess certain characteristics which no one had been able to express in mathematical terms. When he saw the plate spinning and noticed how it wobbled, he immediately wondered if electrons might not act in much the same way. Perhaps their spin was also accompanied by a wobble? So he worked out an amazing new theory based on this novel idea. It proved to be so significant that it earned him the Nobel Prize.

Not everybody has the humility to see the world the way Feynman did. He had the awareness to appreciate that life has a great deal to offer provided we approach it with a genuine sense of wonder and inquiry.

4
Using the Spiritual Exercises of ECK to Connect with the Holy Spirit

How the Spiritual Exercises of ECK Get Results

The Living ECK Master teaches spiritual exercises which harness your creativity and channel it in a wholly new direction. When we focus on the Light and Sound, the twin aspects of the Holy Spirit, we enable this divine force to flow forth from within. In a very real sense we are issuing an invitation to God to assist us in our unfoldment. And even though we might not recognize it at first, God responds.

As we grow in consciousness, we may begin to hear one of the many sounds of the Holy Spirit or see an inner light. This light may be a soft or pastel shade of blue, lavender, pink, orange, or yellow, depending on the inner

plane you are attuned to. The appearance of a Blue Star, like a soft globe or a point of sparkling blue light, denotes the presence of the Mahanta.

Many who have had near-death experiences report seeing a bright inner light. This is the light of Divine Spirit, the same light one sees during contemplation using the Spiritual Exercises of ECK.

I believe that many children love Christmas trees, with their brightly colored lights, because they remind them of the world they lived in before they were born.

One of the most popular exercises in Eckankar is based on HU, an ancient name for God. Just as the Absolute has a different name in each language, for example *Dieu* in French, *Dios* in Spanish, or *God* in English, It was known in ancient times as *HU*. The sound of HU is very special. The great spiritual Masters say it comes from the inner planes and may be found in the many sounds of nature. While repetition of the sacred syllable *Aum* will lead in time to the Mental Plane, the imperishable sound *HU* will lift the individual completely beyond the lower worlds, to the Soul Plane and beyond.

Dreams, a Doorway to Heaven

Your inner faculties are like the muscles in your physical body. The more you exercise them, the stronger they become. A daily spiritual exercise is like a workout. As the weeks and months go by, you will become more spiritually aware and your personal creativity will increase. You will also become more receptive to the Light and Sound and the way they are working in your life.

One of the earliest benefits, and one which many students experience, is a more productive and rewarding dream life. Even seekers who have no recall of their dreams report a marked improvement after starting the Spiritual Exercises of ECK. Everyone dreams, even if they have no recall of their inner journeys. The divine syllable *HU* infuses our inner being with greater light and clarity. As a result, the confused and garbled images of old give way to a series of rich and fulfilling dream experiences.

There are many kinds of dreams. Some help you work off karma from previous lives—an extremely important benefit for anyone striving to achieve a higher state of consciousness. Many students report visits to inner temples and schools, and conversations with the ECK Masters who teach there. Some dreams shed light on problems which are facing us in daily life—how to resolve a situation at work, sort out a domestic difficulty, find a successful course of treatment for a

persistent illness, and so forth. Other dreams lift us in full consciousness to realms which we are not yet ready to enter via contemplation. These experiences can bring an influx of Divine Spirit in the form of Light and Sound, a cleansing process which greatly aids in our spiritual purification.

Other students report meeting loved ones who have passed over, even family pets who have left the physical and are now living on one of the inner planes.

A lively dream life is a very significant boon to anyone in search of God. It literally opens up new worlds. Vistas we hardly ever imagined begin to flow very gently into our waking awareness. Instead of seeing ourselves as a physical body with a spiritual dimension, we begin to see ourselves as Soul with—for the time being—a physical body. The fear of death begins to lose its grip, including the subconscious shadow it casts over the lives and motivation of so many today.

Sharing Your Love with All Life

Perhaps the most remarkable benefit of all is found when we start to love ourselves as Soul. To know that God loves us is intellectually satisfying, but to be aware of this as a living reality in our daily life is rewarding beyond measure. When we reach this point, we start to love ourselves also, as well as Soul in everyone we meet.

With this comes the leap from self-service to God service. The old goals, which once seemed so important, are replaced by a higher set of ideals. Many students say that when this happens, they start to enjoy life as never before. The deep purpose in the world around them begins to shine forth. They know where they are going and the steps they must take to get there. Most important of all, they know that a life built around service to oneself alone is both cold and empty, a karmic treadmill which leads nowhere.

Some years ago scientists in the Arabian desert were studying how the indigenous wildlife survived in such a hot, inhospitable environment. The temperature at midday often exceeded 120 degrees Fahrenheit. With no trees or shrubs, there was hardly any shade where small birds could find cover. They discovered that one species of bird had solved the problem in a very original way. Another desert inhabitant, a small lizard, lived in a deep burrow. For some reason he didn't seem to mind if the bird snuggled inside for a few hours every day to shelter from the sun. The cooler temperature inside the burrow—not to mention the lizard's generous nature—enabled the bird to survive.

The scientists were puzzled by one thing though. There was never more than one bird inside the burrow at any one time. Continuing their observations, they learned that whenever a second bird tried to enter, the first bird always threw him out, even though there was still plenty of room.

Perhaps the lizard understood a spiritual law which the bird had yet to learn.

5
Accepting the Assistance of the Living ECK Master

The Purpose of the Living ECK Master

Despite appearances, you are an ancient spiritual being. Just about every person on earth today has had many past lives in the human form. Before reentering the physical body, each individual Soul had a consultation with Its spiritual counselor or "guardian angel" to select an incarnation best suited to Its needs. Some chose a male body, others a female. Sometimes we choose a challenging life in order to have the kind of experiences which will enable us to develop spiritually in one direction or another. At other times we may choose an uneventful lifetime, to catch our breath as it were, or perhaps a lifetime which ends in an early death. (Of course, we already knew before we entered the lifetime in question that it would be short. The big details in each lifetime are planned well in advance).

The purpose of the Mahanta, the Living ECK Master is to assist those Souls who are ready to make a big leap spiritually. In a sense, they are pulling together the strengths and talents which they have acquired over many lifetimes and forging a wholly new outlook on life, an outlook centered entirely on the Light and Sound of God.

Thus Eckankar is like a finishing school for students preparing for graduation. The first stage in our graduation is known as Self-Realization, while another is known as God-Realization.

Some skills we acquire intuitively, while others must be taught. In many ways we are like the Red-Crowned Japanese Crane. This wonderful bird has been revered by the Japanese for generations, and like all birds, it must be taught how to fly.

In one nature reserve, where low-lying nests are often inundated by rising flood waters, the keeper must retrieve the eggs from any abandoned nests and try to hatch them himself. This is a laborious process, taking many weeks. He places them in an incubator and carefully monitors the temperature, listening all the while for any sign that they may be ready to hatch.

When he hears a little tapping sound, he knows they are about to break forth. But he does not help them at

this stage. Instead he places the egg on a table and watches as the helpless little creatures struggle for several hours to extract themselves from their sturdy shells. He knows they must do this if they are to develop the strength they will need to survive. Next, he spends hours, even days, getting them to accept the little minnows and worms which form an essential part of their diet.

All of this love and care would come to naught if these beautiful birds never learned to fly. So the keeper shows them how. When they are about three months old, he leads them to a long meadow and runs up and down flapping his arms. At first the bird has no idea what all of this means. But as the days pass the bird starts to imitate the keeper, and before long it is airborne!

The Mahanta is just like the keeper, teaching each of his students how to unfold their golden wings and soar above the limitations of the human condition.

The Rhythm of Life

Many seekers are troubled by the knowledge that evil exists. Why, they reason, would a just and loving God allow evil to hold sway in the world? They have forgotten the Law of Karma which we have already mentioned. This law insures that only the effects which we have set in motion ourselves can enter our lives. Nothing we have earned can be kept from us. Viewed in this light, the world is totally just. Everything is in its right place.

If difficulties exist in our life, they are simply a reflection of our past actions and our existing state of consciousness. By working through them, we can restore balance to our lives and lay the foundation for future growth.

It is our accumulated good karma over many lifetimes which eventually earns us the opportunity to meet and study with the Living ECK Master.

Through a clear understanding of the ancient laws and daily practice of the Spiritual Exercises of ECK we can find a deep inner harmony. The Holy Spirit is Itself the rhythm of life. When we harmonize with this great force, we gradually come into harmony with everything around us.

The Renaissance artist Raphael had a joyful life. His paintings profoundly affected his contemporaries and many traveled great distances just to view his work. He also possessed what might be described as a talent for harmony. It was said that he never ceased to show others how to conduct themselves well, regardless of their station.

Even craftsmen, who were swayed by petty jealousies and base thoughts, and who frequently bickered and quarreled with each other, would dwell in a state of natural harmony and agreement when he was among them.

Because of this, his dignified behavior and loving kindness were said to rival his great accomplishments on canvas.

The Mahanta, the Living ECK Master encourages his students to attend regular spiritual classes known as Satsang where they can study the writings of Eckankar in a group setting. These special classes, which normally take place once a month, help to stimulate their spiritual awareness and promote a greater personal understanding of the ancient laws of ECK.

To assist the student in his or her unfoldment, the Living ECK Master provides monthly discourses. These are studied at home by the individual and can be reviewed each month in a Satsang class.

Before embarking on her illustrious career, the great opera singer Maria Callas studied voice in Athens. As an unknown student, she arrived every morning at 10:00 a.m. for her half-hour lesson. Other students would normally head off after their lesson, but not Callas. Instead she brought along a packed lunch and stayed the whole day, watching each and every student as they went through their paces. As she explained, "I felt that even the least talented pupil could teach me something."

No matter where you are in your unfoldment, Eckankar will lift you to a higher level.

Sri Harold Klemp
The Mahanta,
the Living ECK Master

6
Uncovering the Totality through Eckankar

An Individual Path

Eckankar is an individual path. You can study it alone if you wish. You can even continue with your existing religion if you feel this may be necessary for family or other reasons. Your relationship with Divine Spirit is entirely a personal matter. Nobody can tell you how to live your life. God has given each of us complete freedom to make our own way home, in our own time. Eckankar is therefore a gift to the individual. It shortens the homeward journey and makes it easier for the sincere seeker to unravel the mysteries of life.

In learning who we really are, we will make many extraordinary discoveries. For example, there are

untold benefits in recognizing the distinction between mind and Soul. Where mind often struggles for power, status, and pleasure, and thereby dominates the lives of most people today, Soul interacts with the world in a much more fulfilling and rewarding way.

When the Light and Sound of God go to work in your consciousness they bring about a purification which opens your heart. This in turn fosters a deep appreciation of all that is taking place for our benefit.

The Unity of Life

Through daily practice of the Spiritual Exercises of ECK, we start to see life as a whole, as something vastly more than the sum of it parts. And when this happens our outlook is transformed.

Leonardo da Vinci was once commissioned by the pope to portray a particular subject on canvas. He immediately set about distilling the necessary oils to prepare the varnish needed to coat the finished work. When he heard this, the pope is said to have exclaimed: "Oh dear, this man will never do anything. He is thinking about finishing the work before he even starts it!"

To accomplish anything of value, we must live as though it has already been achieved. Only then will it come to pass. By preparing the varnish in advance, Leonardo was reminding himself of this ancient spiritual law.

The Living ECK Master helps the student to remember what he came into this world to achieve. What's more, the Master sets in motion a series of experiences, based on the student's individual karma, which raise his consciousness step-by-step to a much higher level. These will lead in time to that unthinkable unity or wholeness—God Itself.

Today there is great interest in psychic phenomena and things of this nature. While this is neither good nor bad in itself, it can distract the seeker from his true goal in life.

Until we connect with the Holy Spirit, and perceive It through our inner faculties in the form of the Light and Sound of God, we are prey to the many illusions which dog the human condition. For every one we see and avoid, there are many more which work away in silence and continue to hold us back spiritually. Until we make a deliberate effort to unfold consciously, it simply won't happen.

When a young journalist got a chance to interview a great Russian violinist, he jumped at the opportunity. "How wonderful it must be," he remarked, "to be able to pick up your violin any time you want and hear the most beautiful music."

She smiled indulgently. "But you forget," she said, "that to get to this point I had to listen to myself playing the most dreadful noise for nearly eight years, hour after hour, day after day—to every note!"

If one develops the discipline to listen to the Sound of the Holy Spirit on a daily basis, It will lift him above the turmoil and distractions of the psychic worlds. The prophets of God in earlier generations—such as Jesus, Buddha, Muhammad, and Ramakrishna—all taught their disciples the vital importance of placing their attention every day on the Holy Spirit, since out of this practice alone flow all other blessings.

Today the Mahanta, the Living ECK Master teaches exactly the same message, but in a form suited to the needs of the twenty-first century. He also demonstrates the factors common to all religions—the ancient spiritual laws mentioned earlier—and presents them in a streamlined and modern form, stripped of the many inessentials which burden other religious paths.

The Wayshower

The Living ECK Master is assisted in his work by the ECK Masters, known as the Vairagi Adepts. While a few still retain a physical body here on earth, most are based on the inner planes. These great Adepts help all who are sincere in their desire to travel back home to God. They operate schools in the inner worlds which the student can visit in the dream state, at the invitation of the Living ECK Master.

These schools, many of which are in Temples of Golden Wisdom, provide classes, seminars, and workshops on the ancient doctrines of ECK. They also provide a wide range of spiritual counseling and healing therapies, as well as one-to-one instruction. Many students are blessed with a conscious recall of their visits to these peerless spiritual centers.

Often seekers today have had dreams with one of these ECK Masters, or perhaps a vision or an actual encounter in the physical world. These experiences generally bring a wonderful feeling of upliftment or a clear sense that something of great spiritual significance has just taken place. Many people have a guardian angel, but the ECK Masters work from an even higher level. An encounter with one of these great Adepts is very special indeed.

The Mahanta, the Living ECK Master is the Wayshower. He helps the seeker make contact with the Light and Sound of God and, in the course of his unfoldment, introduces him to other ECK Masters for training in specific aspects of truth. Seen in this way, the Living ECK Master is the focal point for all who seek to transcend the human state of consciousness and start their sacred journey to the Soul Plane and beyond.

Prior to 1884 the geography of the world was set out in maps which had no internationally agreed point of reference. Some centered on Rome or Jerusalem or another well-known location, but this often led to serious errors when information was being transferred between maps. So a large number of countries settled on Greenwich in London as the common point of reference for all maps. As a result global travel was considerably simplified and many longstanding pitfalls were removed.

The Mahanta, the Living ECK Master is like a meridian line for the seeker, a central point of reference on his journey home to God.

7
Finding Divine Guidance in Everyday Life

The Mahanta as the Guardian of the Path

The ECK Masters in every age have striven to protect the purity of these teachings. In a sense, the ECK doctrine is like an intricate piece of software. Once bugs start to creep in, it can no longer function as intended.

The Living ECK Master steers the seeker away from beliefs and practices which only slow him down. These include ascetic practices, elaborate dietary rules, hours of daily meditation, and a monastic lifestyle. On the other hand he highlights the responsibilities of family life, service to the community, and the many spiritual opportunities to be found in the workplace.

The spiritual student's first responsibility is to his family and loved ones. For example, if a person wishes to practice Eckankar but his or her partner in marriage is opposed to the idea, then they should discuss the matter in a loving way and agree on a course which is acceptable to both of them.

As the guardian of the path, the Mahanta, the Living ECK Master endeavors to make the ancient teachings of Eckankar available to as wide an audience as possible. Eckankar is not a secret path but a fount of wisdom and knowledge with something for everyone. Neither does it claim to be the only path to God, just the most direct.

The Living ECK Master presents truth in its purest form to all who are ready to receive it. However, many who find truth try to turn it to their own advantage. Instead of sharing it with others, they seek to exploit it for personal gain, recognition, or social standing. After repeating this error over many lifetimes, Soul finally learns the imperishable splendor of selfless service, of passing on the fruits of what we have received.

Overcoming the Fear of Death

Soul incarnates so often in the human form that It starts to identify with the body. Just about every civilization and religion has striven to address the problems which this creates. Through daily practice of the Spiritual Exercises of ECK, we begin to reexperience awareness as Soul, independent of the physical body. This awareness is generally very gentle at first, akin to a dream. But as our consciousness expands, the reality of our beingness as Soul becomes easier to perceive.

In his remarkable book *The Tiger's Fang,* Paul Twitchell describes a journey he took through the inner worlds in the company of his guide and teacher, the ECK Master Rebazar Tarzs. Paul was amazed by what he saw. The farther he traveled from the earth plane, the more he struggled to comprehend the splendor and vastness of the worlds beyond.

Soul can never die, and as we explore the inner worlds via Soul Travel, the fear of death loses its grip.

At the same time, our inner explorations will teach us to cherish the lessons and experiences which our latest incarnation is now offering and to seek every opportunity to further our unfoldment until the natural cycle of our life is complete.

In 1917, Lawrence of Arabia and a companion were making their way by camel from Azrak to Bair when they were surprised in the desert by four armed bandits and ordered to dismount. Since the ruthless quartet would almost certainly have cut them down without mercy, Lawrence simply ignored their command and proceeded to *laugh* at them. The surly thugs were amazed by this audacity.

Lawrence then hailed the ringleader over, leaned forward in his saddle and whispered an odious insult into his ear, the kind of remark which would normally have guaranteed immediate death. The ringleader was so taken aback by this impertinence that he began to wonder whether his intended victim had support hidden in the surrounding hills. At that moment, Lawrence rode slowly away, instructing his companion to do likewise. They had just enough time to make their escape before the startled bandits recovered their wits.

An incident like this would suggest that Lawrence had long passed the point where the threat of death could dampen his enthusiasm for life.

The Art of Living

God sent Soul into the lower worlds to master the art of living. We learn this best by giving and receiving love and by doing the things we love. Then, if we allow it, the Holy Spirit will guide us in the direction best suited to our individual needs. Whether or not we pay attention and heed what life is telling us is entirely our own choice.

The great strength of the Spiritual Exercises of ECK is that they make it easier for the student to perceive the hand of Divine Spirit in his daily affairs and to direct his efforts accordingly.

While out walking one day, a young man stopped to watch a heron fishing on the shore of a broad river. For some reason the bird was running up and down the shore in a seemingly random fashion, stabbing at the water as he went. The young man also noticed a cormorant fishing in the middle of the river, diving and surfacing every half minute or so.

The heron appeared to be watching the ripples in the water that the cormorant made as it dived for fish.

This unusual cycle of activity went on for some time. The young man finally guessed what was happening.

Whenever the cormorant sliced down through the water, he disturbed the fish in that part of the river, so they swam toward the shore to avoid him. The heron seemed to know that wherever the cormorant went along the river, the fish would congregate near the shore opposite that point.

The student, too, learns to move through life like the watchful heron, ever aware of the gentle and often unseen ways in which the Mahanta channels the blessings of heaven in his direction. It is only through daily practice of the Spiritual Exercises of ECK that he develops the awareness needed to perceive these golden opportunities.

8
The History and Purpose of Eckankar

The Origin of the Human Race

Science teaches that the universe began with the Big Bang, a massive expansion of mass and energy from a central point, a singularity. Out of this the stars formed. Like enormous nuclear reactors, they synthesized the hydrogen and helium from the Big Bang to produce the elements essential to life, such as

carbon, nitrogen, and oxygen. Some stars superheated and exploded, producing the planets, comets, and other cosmic phenomena.

The Big Bang is believed to have occurred about twelve billion years ago, while the Earth is thought to have formed four to five billion years ago. Through a long process of evolution, many different life-forms emerged, most of which are now extinct. After the dinosaurs disappeared about sixty-five million years ago, the many species of mammal began to develop and occupy prominent niches in the planet's ecosystem. Modern primates became established some seven million years ago, while the species *homo sapiens* is believed to have emerged just two hundred thousand years ago in the Rift Valley in the east coast of Africa.

Scientists have great difficulty seeing the many causes which combined over time to produce the amazing universe we all live in today. There is a guiding intelligence behind evolution which science has yet to discover. Nothing really happens by chance. The ECK Masters have long taught that the physical plane is just one level of reality and that others exist at higher vibratory rates.

Anything which manifests here on earth has first existed at a higher level. Thus, while humans evolved from other animal forms, they did so in accordance

with a divine plan. Similar intelligent life-forms have also evolved on many other planets in solar systems remote from this one.

The ECK Masters teach that it is not our human form which makes us children of God. Soul incarnates in the human body to gain a range of experiences which are not readily obtainable in other animal forms.

We are spiritual because we are Soul and not because we are human. However, our lessons in the human body help us to advance into higher levels of spiritual awareness.

The Living ECK Master invites all seekers to rejoice in the opportunity which life is now offering. By setting our sights on God-Realization, we can finish the cycles of rebirth and graduate to one of the higher levels of reality. The whole purpose of Eckankar is to show how this can be achieved.

There are eight outer initiations in Eckankar. These are normally spaced a number of years apart to allow the individual to grow at his own pace. The First Initiation occurs in the dream state during one's first year of membership, while the second is given in an outer ceremony at the start of his third year. All other initiations are given in their own time as we pass certain milestones in our unfoldment.

A Short History of Eckankar

The word *Eckankar* means "Co-worker with God." This is the goal of all Souls, whether they are aware of it or not. The teachings of ECK have been on this planet for millennia, though they have seldom been taught openly. Paul Twitchell brought them to the public in 1965. There are many parallels between other religious teachings and Eckankar. However, Eckankar, as taught by the Living ECK Master, predates all of them. Rumi, the remarkable Sufi poet of the thirteenth century, was a follower of ECK, as was Milarepa, the venerable Tibetan sage of the twelfth century. Eckankar, as we know it today, was last taught openly by the ECK Master Gopal Das, who was responsible for the writing of the Egyptian Book of Dreams around 3000 B.C.

Many students of Eckankar today can recall working with the ECK Masters who upheld this ancient teaching in the fabled continents of Atlantis and Lemuria some tens of thousands of years ago.

How Does Eckankar Compare with Christianity?

Eckankar today is the Religion of the Light and Sound of God. It does not claim to be the only path to God, just the most direct. It recognizes the need for a diversity of religious paths to serve the many different levels of consciousness which exist in the world. No single religion can fit everybody.

The ECK Masters teach that Soul is not lost, therefore there is no need for a savior in the traditional sense. However, the Living ECK Master, like Jesus, Buddha, and the prophets of earlier times, is authorized by God to provide the spiritual guidance needed by seekers of truth.

The ECK Masters also place great emphasis on the principle of personal responsibility. We can only learn by paying our debts to life. Hence no priest or holy man can wipe the slate clean in a confessional or through deathbed absolution. We are accountable at all times for our behavior, for our deeds and for our thoughts.

Christianity, along with several other world religions, has made its heaven or paradise on the Mental Plane. This is a region of such splendor that the mystics who bring back reports of life on that level are often at a loss to describe what they have seen. But the Soul Plane is higher still. Soul can only graduate from the lower worlds and thereby terminate the cycles of reincarnation by becoming established on the Soul Plane. It behooves us, therefore, to aim as high as we can and to order our lives accordingly.

The Living ECK Master is both the inner and outer teacher for his students. The outer teachers of most

religions today do not have this spiritual capacity. This means the followers must look exclusively to their departed founders, saints, and prophets for inner guidance and protection. While this can give a general direction to their lives, it cannot provide the individualized guidance and training needed to transcend the boundaries of the lower worlds and become established on the Soul Plane.

The Eckankar Organization

Like other religious organizations, Eckankar has an administrative structure to assist with spiritual programs, coordinate the printing and distribution of books and discourses, and to handle membership records. This is located in Minneapolis, Minnesota. Eckankar also holds annual seminars and has a global network of spiritually trained volunteers who assist the Living ECK Master in his work. Running costs are kept to a minimum. There are no hidden fees or overheads, and there is no charge of any kind for the ECK initiation. Unfoldment comes only through spiri-

tual merit and is entirely a personal matter between the individual and Divine Spirit.

Members receive monthly discourses written by the Living ECK Master. The inner rhythm of these monthly communications is specially tuned to the needs of the seeker and will assist him greatly in expanding his awareness.

The spiritual home of Eckankar is the Temple of ECK in Chanhassen, Minnesota (just outside Minneapolis), completed in 1990. The Temple of ECK is a sacred place which seekers of all religions may visit to pray and contemplate. By their own accounts, many students have received spiritual blessings and revelatory experiences while visiting the Temple. The Living ECK Master has described the Temple as "a way station between the physical and the spiritual worlds . . . a gathering place for inner and outer study."

9
Some Frequently Asked Questions

Does Eckankar claim to be the only path to God?
There are many paths to God, and Eckankar is one of them. Eckankar does claim, however, to be the most direct path to God.

Does Eckankar come from India?
The ECK teachings have been on this planet since the dawn of time, in one form or another. No country can claim to be their birthplace. However, they have seldom been taught as openly as they have been since Eckankar's founder, Paul Twitchell, brought them forth in their modern form in the mid–twentieth century.

Do Eckankar members worship the Living ECK Master?
Eckankar members have deep respect for the Living ECK Master, but they do not worship him. All ECK Masters discourage emotional dependency upon, or attachment to, a personality.

Who appoints the Living ECK Master?
The Living ECK Master is chosen by the Sugmad (God). Every Living ECK Master trains his successor.

Who is the current Living ECK Master?
The current Living ECK Master is Sri Harold Klemp. He became the Mahanta, the Living ECK Master in 1981.

How many planes are there?

There are countless planes and subplanes. The lower worlds include the Physical, Astral, Causal, Mental, and Etheric Planes. The first plane beyond the lower worlds is known as the Soul Plane. There are many planes above that as well.

Is Soul Travel the same as astral travel?

No. Astral travel is a cumbersome and limited method of leaving the body. Soul Travel is much easier to learn and works in a completely different way, expanding one's consciousness with the Light and Sound of God. Astral travel is confined to the Astral Plane, while Soul Travel can take one all the way to the Soul Plane.

Is it possible to work off all one's karma in one lifetime?

Yes. The program of unfoldment overseen by the Living ECK Master enables the student to work through his karma and complete his training here on earth before moving on to the next world. Much of this karmic burn-off occurs in the dream state, sometimes on several levels at once. This is a major benefit for all who are seeking to establish a foothold in the high worlds of God.

Will Eckankar make my life easier?

The purpose of Eckankar is to help you forge a closer working relationship with the Holy Spirit. This brings understanding, wisdom, love, and a host of spiritual tools to better deal with life's challenges.

Does Eckankar have clergy? If so, how do they qualify?

Members who have reached the higher initiations—Fifth and above—may qualify for Eckankar clergy. The spiritual training for this position can generally take fifteen to twenty years. Eckankar clergy perform a range of sacerdotal functions and serve in the community on a voluntary, nonremunerated basis.

Does Eckankar aim to bring about world peace?

The ECK Masters remind their students that the physical world is a melting pot of many kinds of experience with Souls of varying degrees of maturity. This is how God designed it. Eckankar aims only to assist Soul on Its journey back to God.

Is Eckankar an offshoot of another religion?

No. While scholars may debate this at length and arrive at different conclusions, the fundamentals of Eckankar have their basis in antiquity. The ECK Masters have worked in every part of the world at various stages throughout history and have influenced the evolution of many other religious paths.

Does Eckankar have any rules or restrictions such as a dress code or dietary guidelines?

There are no rules or restrictions of this kind in Eckankar. However, students are expected to observe the highest standard of ethics and personal behavior.

Cigarette smoking and the drinking of alcohol are discouraged. The use of drugs other than for medical treatment is seen as a step backward in spiritual unfoldment and is strongly discouraged.

Does Eckankar oppose abortion or homosexuality?

Eckankar teaches that Soul is immortal and that It is here on earth to gain experience. Eckankar considers such matters as abortion, divorce, or sexual orientation to be individual decisions and, as an organization, takes no stance.

Does Eckankar have a holy book?

Yes. It is known as *The Shariyat-Ki-Sugmad,* which means "Way of the Eternal," and comprises about twelve volumes. The first two volumes have been published, while the remaining volumes may be consulted on the inner planes.

Is Eckankar expensive to follow?

No. Eckankar requests a membership donation with each year of membership. The suggested donation in 2002 was $130 for an individual or $160 for a family in a developed country ($50 for an individual and $75 for a family in developing countries).

Can I study Eckankar in the privacy of my own home?

Yes. Some members choose to study the ECK discourses privately and have little contact with other members.

Can I practice Eckankar without becoming a member?

Yes. The Mahanta, the Living ECK Master will work spiritually with all seekers who look to him for guidance and protection. However, the ECK initiations and the special program of training provided by the Living ECK Master are only available to seekers who select Eckankar as their spiritual path and become members.

Can members leave Eckankar at their own choosing?

Yes. To hold anyone to a particular path against their will is a serious violation of spiritual law.

10
A Spiritual Exercise to Try at Home

The following exercise has been taught by the ECK Masters for thousands of years. It is designed to open your heart to divine love.

Begin by sitting comfortably in a quiet place where you won't be disturbed. Next, close your eyes, and place your attention at the center of your forehead. This is the location of the Spiritual Eye, the natural resting place for Soul in the human body.

Then, on the outgoing breath, sing the word *HU,* an ancient, sacred name for God (which sounds just like the English word *hue*). As you do this, know that God loves and accepts you exactly as you are. Be aware that God's love allows you to exist. Continue to sing *HU* in a soft voice, with love.

By doing this simple exercise for about ten minutes every day, you may begin to notice a change in your inner life or in your general outlook. Many have reported hearing an inner sound, like the sound of the wind or falling rain or another sound of nature. One may also see an inner light or a soothing glow. These are the Light and Sound of God, the twin aspects of the Holy Spirit.

Some seekers also experience a gentle inner movement, a subtle shift in consciousness known as Soul Travel. This can seem like a dream at first, but a dream of a special kind. This is the movement of Soul beyond the body to another plane of consciousness. It is God's way of bringing about the purification needed for entry into a higher level of spiritual awareness.

11
Next Steps

If you are interested in learning more about Eckankar, you can read one or more books written by the Mahanta, the Living ECK Master, Sri Harold Klemp. You can also contact your local Eckankar center (check the phonebook) or write to ECKANKAR, P.O. Box 27300, Minneapolis, MN 55427 U.S.A. for further information on books, membership, or local contacts.

Eckankar has a very informative Web site at www.eckankar.org. The Web site also contains links to other Eckankar Web sites around the world.

If you live in the United States or Canada, you can call the toll-free number 1-800-LOVE GOD for free information.

Interested persons can also attend ECK Worship Services, workshops, or Eckankar discussion classes to get a further understanding of this ancient path and to see whether it is likely to meet their spiritual needs.

Membership includes a set of twelve monthly discourses written by the Living ECK Master; a quarterly magazine, the *Mystic World* (which has regular articles by the Living ECK Master); and other information relating to seminars and new publications.

New members receive the First Initiation in Eckankar from the Mahanta—the inner side of the Mahanta, the Living ECK Master—in the dream state. This is normally given during the first year of membership. They are then eligible to request the Second Initiation in Eckankar at the end of their second year of membership. This is given by an authorized representative of the Living ECK Master.

All who become members of Eckankar grow aware of the love and protection of the Mahanta, the Living ECK Master.

12
The Age-Old Quest for Divine Love and Spiritual Freedom

"No one on earth moves in a direct line toward a goal of any sort. We zigzag. We go up and down the hills, we go left and right, we take little detours. This is true whether we're trying to find our way back home to God or whether we're trying to learn how to live a fruitful life in this lifetime, to better ourselves, to be worth something. So that when our time comes to go, people will say, 'He was a good man' or 'She was a good woman.'

"What made us that? Essentially, it's as the New Testament says, 'God is love.' And as we say in Eckankar, Soul exists because God loves It. That means you exist because God loves you. This is the essence of truth. This is the heart of any teaching."

—Harold Klemp, *Our Spiritual Wake-up Calls,* Mahanta Transcripts, Book 15

Glossary

Words set in SMALL CAPS are defined elsewhere in this glossary.

ECK. *EHK* The Life Force, the Holy Spirit, or Audible Life Current which sustains all life.

ECKANKAR. *EHK-ahn-kahr* Religion of the Light and Sound of God. Also known as the Ancient Science of SOUL TRAVEL. A truly spiritual religion for the individual in modern times. The teachings provide a framework for anyone to explore their own spiritual experiences. Established by Paul Twitchell, the modern-day founder, in 1965. The word means "Co-worker with God."

ECK MASTERS. Spiritual Masters who can assist and protect people in their spiritual studies and travels. The ECK Masters are from a long line of God-Realized SOULS who know the responsibility that goes with spiritual freedom.

GOD-REALIZATION. The state of God Consciousness. Complete and conscious awareness of God.

HU. *HYOO* The most ancient, secret name for God. The singing of the word HU is considered a love song to God. It can be sung aloud or silently to oneself.

INITIATION. Earned by a member of ECKANKAR through spiritual unfoldment and service to God. The initiation is a private ceremony in which the individual is linked to the Sound and Light of God.

LIVING ECK MASTER. The title of the spiritual leader of ECKANKAR. His duty is to lead SOULS back to God. The Living ECK Master can assist spiritual students physically as the Outer Master, in the dream state as the Dream Master, and in the spiritual worlds as the Inner Master. Sri Harold Klemp became the MAHANTA, the Living ECK Master in 1981.

MAHANTA. *mah-HAHN-tah* A title to describe the highest state of God Consciousness on earth, often embodied in the LIVING ECK MASTER. He is the Living Word. An expression of the Spirit of God that is always with you.

Planes. The levels of existence, such as the Physical, Astral, Causal, Mental, Etheric, and Soul Planes.

Satsang. *SAHT-sahng* A class in which students of ECK study a monthly lesson from Eckankar.

Self-Realization. Soul recognition. The entering of Soul into the Soul Plane and there beholding Itself as pure Spirit. A state of seeing, knowing, and being.

The Shariyat-Ki-Sugmad. *SHAH-ree-aht-kee-SOOG-mahd* The sacred scriptures of Eckankar. The scriptures are comprised of twelve volumes in the spiritual worlds. The first two were transcribed from the inner planes by Paul Twitchell, modern-day founder of Eckankar.

Soul. The True Self. The inner, most sacred part of each person. Soul exists before birth and lives on after the death of the physical body. As a spark of God, Soul can see, know, and perceive all things. It is the creative center of Its own world.

Soul Travel. The expansion of consciousness. The ability of Soul to transcend the physical body and travel into the spiritual worlds of God. Soul Travel is taught only by the Living ECK Master. It helps people unfold spiritually and can provide proof of the existence of God and life after death.

Sound and Light of ECK. The Holy Spirit. The two aspects through which God appears in the lower worlds. People can experience them by looking and listening within themselves and through Soul Travel.

Spiritual Exercises of ECK. The daily practice of certain techniques to get us in touch with the Light and Sound of God.

Sri. *SREE* A title of spiritual respect, similar to reverend or pastor, used for those who have attained the kingdom of God. In Eckankar, it is reserved for the Mahanta, the Living ECK Master.

Sugmad. *SOOG-mahd* A sacred name for God. Sugmad is neither masculine nor feminine; It is the source of all life.

For more explanations of Eckankar terms, see *A Cosmic Sea of Words: The ECKANKAR Lexicon* by Harold Klemp.

For Further Reading and Study

The Spiritual Laws of Life
Harold Klemp

There exist truths—spiritual laws that guide and benefit us. How can we shape our lives and destiny to live in harmony with them? Discover how you can meet today's challenges in a more relaxed, awakened, and happy way. The spiritual laws of life give us many resources to make the very best decisions at any one moment in our life.

Past Lives, Dreams, and Soul Travel
Harold Klemp

What if you could recall past-life lessons for advantage today? You knew dreams are real, another way to find wisdom from the heart? And via Soul Travel, a shift in consciousness, you could tap into wisdom and knowledge of the last great frontier—to fully, consciously ride the wave of divine love coming into your life every day? Harold Klemp, a leading authority on all three subjects, shows you how.

This book can help you find your true purpose, greater love than you've ever known, and spiritual freedom.

How to Survive Spiritually in Our Times, Mahanta Transcripts, Book 16
Harold Klemp

A master storyteller, Harold Klemp weaves stories, tips, and techniques into the golden fabric of his talks. They highlight the deeper truths within you, so you can apply them in your life *now*. He speaks right to Soul. It is that divine, eternal spark that you are. The survivor. Yet survival is only the starting point in your spiritual life. Harold Klemp also shows you how to gain in spiritual wealth. This book's a treasure.

Autobiography of a Modern Prophet
Harold Klemp

Master your true destiny. Learn how this man's journey to God illuminates the way for you too. Dare to explore the outer limits of the last great frontier, your spiritual worlds! The more you explore them, the sooner you come to discovering your true nature as an infinite, eternal spark of God. This book helps you get there! A good read.

The Art of Spiritual Dreaming
Harold Klemp

Dreams are a treasure. A gift from God. Harold Klemp shows how to find a dream's spiritual gold, and how to experience God's love. Get insights from the past and future, grow in confidence, and make decisions about career and finances. Do this from a unique perspective: by recognizing the spiritual nature of your dreams.

A Modern Prophet Answers Your Key Questions about Life
Harold Klemp

A pioneer of today's focus on "everyday spirituality" shows you how to experience and understand God's love in your life—anytime, anyplace. His answers to hundreds of questions help guide you to your own source of wisdom, peace, and deep inner joy.

The Tiger's Fang
Paul Twitchell

Paul Twitchell's teacher, Rebazar Tarzs, takes him on a journey through vast worlds of Light and Sound, to sit at the feet of the spiritual Masters. Their conversations bring out the secret of how to draw closer to God—and awaken Soul to Its spiritual destiny. Many have used this book, with its vivid descriptions of heavenly worlds and citizens, to begin their own spiritual adventures.

35 Golden Keys to Who You Are & Why You're Here
Linda C. Anderson

Discover thirty-five golden keys to mastering your spiritual destiny through the ancient teachings of Eckankar, Religion of the Light and Sound of God. The dramatic, true stories in this book equal anything found in the spiritual literature of today. Learn ways to immediately bring more love, peace, and purpose to your life.

Available at your local bookstore. If unavailable, call (952) 380-2222. Or write: ECKANKAR, Dept. BK43, P.O. Box 27300, Minneapolis, MN 55427 U.S.A.

Discover spiritual truth through past lives, dreams, and Soul Travel
Free Eckankar book reveals how

A seeker from New York wrote, "I received your packet and read your book, which was extremely helpful to me. Thank you."

Hundreds of thousands of people around the globe have read *ECKANKAR—Ancient Wisdom for Today* in more than eleven languages. And so many have benefited spiritually.

A Florida newspaper praised this book: "Fascinating and well worth reading as you bring deeper spiritual insight into your life."

You'll see how **past lives** affect every aspect of your life. The way you handle relationships. Make choices. Face challenges.

You'll learn through your own experience that **dreams** are real. They help you make better decisions. Lose the fear of dying—and living — by understanding them.

Using a special technique, you'll find how **Soul Travel** is a natural method for intuitively seeing the big picture and discover spiritual truth for yourself. Begin the adventure of a lifetime *today*.

To get your free copy of *ECKANKAR—Ancient Wisdom for Today* (a $4.95 value), go to Eckankar's Web site at

www.eckankar.org

or call 1-800-LOVE GOD

(1-800-568-3463)

toll free, 24 hours a day. Ask for book #BK43.

Or you can write to: ECKANKAR, Dept. BK43, P.O. Box 27300, Minneapolis, MN 55427 U.S.A.

There May Be an Eckankar Study Group near You

Eckankar offers a variety of local and international activities for the spiritual seeker. With hundreds of study groups worldwide, Eckankar is near you! Many areas have Eckankar centers where you can browse through the books in a quiet, unpressured environment, talk with others who share an interest in this ancient teaching, and attend beginning discussion classes on how to gain the attributes of Soul: wisdom, power, love, and freedom.

Around the world, Eckankar study groups offer special one-day or weekend seminars on the basic teachings of Eckankar. For membership information, visit the Eckankar Web site (www.eckankar.org). For the location of the Eckankar center or study group nearest you, click on "Other Eckankar Web sites" for a listing of those areas with Web sites. You're also welcome to check your phone book under **ECKANKAR**; call **(952) 380-2222, Ext. BK43;** or write **ECKANKAR, Att: Information, BK43, P.O. Box 27300, Minneapolis, MN 55427 U.S.A.**

☐ Please send me information on the nearest Eckankar center or study group in my area.

☐ Please send me more information about membership in Eckankar, which includes a twelve-month spiritual study.

Please type or print clearly

Name _____
　　　　first (given)　　　　　　　　last (family)

Street _____ Apt. # _____

City _____ State/Prov. _____

ZIP/Postal Code _____ Country _____